Abbreviations and Signs:

Classified Lists of Those in Most Common Use

- Frederick William Hamilton -

PREFACE

The use of abbreviations and signs is often a convenience and sometimes a temptation. It is a saving of time and labor which is entirely justifiable under certain conditions, one of which is that all such short cuts should be sufficiently conventional and familiar to be intelligible to any person likely to read the printed matter in which they occur. Scientific and technical signs and abbreviations are part of the nomenclature of the subject to which they belong and must be learned by students of it. General readers are not particularly concerned with them.

The use of abbreviations and signs is partly a matter of office style and partly a matter of author's preference. Certain fairly well established rules have, however, emerged from the varieties of usage in vogue. An attempt has been made in the following pages to state these rules clearly and concisely and to illustrate their application.

Classified lists of the most common abbreviations and signs have been inserted and will be found useful for reference and practice. Sources of further information on these points will be found under the head of Supplementary Reading.

CONTENTS

Introduction
General Rules for the Use of Abbreviations
Dates
Time
Other Abbreviations Involving Numerals
Geographical Abbreviations, with List
Abbreviations of Names, with List
Abbreviations of Titles, with List
Sizes of Books
Weights and Measures
Footnotes
Scriptural Abbreviations
Commercial Abbreviations
Miscellaneous Abbreviations
Monetary Signs
Mathematical Signs

MEDICAL SIGNS
ASTRONOMICAL SIGNS
ECCLESIASTICAL SIGNS
PROOFREADER'S SIGNS
GENERAL OBSERVATIONS
SUPPLEMENTARY READING
REVIEW QUESTIONS

ABBREVIATIONS AND SIGNS

INTRODUCTION

The use of abbreviations is as old as the use of alphabets. In inscriptions and on coins and in other places where room is limited they have always been used in order to save space. The words GUILIELMUS QUARTUS DEI GRATIA REX BRITANNIARUM FIDEI DEFENSOR would hardly go around the circumference of a sixpence, three quarters of an inch in diameter. Therefore, we find them written GUILIELMUS IIII D: G: BRITANNIAR: REX F: D: In the manuscript period abbreviations were very extensively used. This was done partly to lighten the great labor of hand copying and partly to effect a double saving of expense, in labor and in costly material. Certain of these abbreviations were in common use and perfectly intelligible. Unfortunately the copyists did not limit their abbreviations to these, but devised others for their own use much to the discomfort of their readers, especially after the lapse of centuries.

The introduction of printing removed the pressing necessity for the extensive use of abbreviations, but the actual use continued much longer than one would think. The early printed books were reproductions of manuscripts. In some cases the earliest were almost forgeries, and were probably intended to be sold as manuscripts. The types were cut in imitation of the handwriting of some well-known scribe and all his mannerisms and peculiarities were faithfully copied. An incidental result was the expansion of fonts of type by the inclusion of a great number of ligatures and of characters indicating the omission or combination of letters. Habit dies hard, and even after the type founders had freed themselves from the tyranny of manuscript printers continued to follow the habits of the copyist. The saving of material and labor still continued to be considered. The methods of abbreviation in use in written matter continued to be followed in print even down to the first quarter of the last century.

The result of all this abbreviation was serious and well-founded complaint about the difficulty of reading books thus printed. De Vinne gives the following astonishing example, said to be taken practically at random from a Latin copy of the Logic of Ockham printed at Paris in 1488.

> "Sic his e fal sm qd ad simplr a e pducibile a Deo g a e silr hic a n e g a n e pducibile a Deo."

These are the abbreviations for Sicut his est fallacia secundum quid ad simpliciter. A est producibile a Deo. Ergo A est. Et similiter hic. A non est. Ergo A non est producibile a Deo.

The best present usage is to use abbreviations very sparingly. Certain recognized abbreviations are used under certain conditions, but generally only under constraint of limited space.

RULES FOR THE USE OF ABBREVIATIONS

I. GENERAL RULES.

Use no contractions or abbreviations in any place where there is room to print the words in full.

All legitimate words should be spelled out in full in text matter, but abbreviations are often needed in book work for footnotes and tables and in commercial work, where many brief forms and signs are used which are commonly understood and are as intelligible as words.

Certain special forms of printing such as market and stock reports, sporting news, price lists, directories, telephone directories, and the like make extensive use of abbreviations and signs. These abbreviations are of very limited use and often of only temporary life. They are not intelligible to general readers and should never be used outside the particular form of composition to which they pertain. De Vinne suggests that in the absence of printed authority (many of these abbreviations not appearing in the dictionary lists) every proofreader would do well to keep a manuscript book of unlisted abbreviations which he has to use repeatedly as a means of securing uniformity of form.

II. DATES.

Dates are not generally abbreviated in regular text matter; *The Declaration of Independence was signed on July the fourth, 1776.* The word *the* is sometimes omitted. The date might be written *July fourth* but never *July four*.

The abbreviations *ult. inst.* and *prox.* with a numeral (meaning *the 25th of last month, the 25th of this month, the 25th of next month*) are often used in letters, but should not be used in print unless the literal reproduction of a letter is intended.

Do not use *st, d, rd,* or *th* after a date given in figures; *August the sixth*, not *August 6th*.

The accepted abbreviations for the months are:

> *Jan.   Apr.   July   Oct.*
> *Feb.   May   Aug.   Nov.*
> *Mar.   June   Sept.   Dec.*

The accepted abbreviations for the days of the week are:

> *Sun.   Tues.   Thurs.   Sat.*
> *Mon.   Wed.   Fri.*

The accepted abbreviations may be used for the months when the day is given, but not when the month and year alone are given;

> *Jan. 15, 1916*, but *January 1916.*

Some good authorities prefer the order day, month, year; *15 Jan., 1916,* but this is a matter of office style. Generally speaking the more common order is the better quite regardless of the logical character because it requires less mental effort on the part of the reader. For example in writing addresses English speaking people put the number before the street, *59 Wall St.,* while others put the number after the street, *Wall St., 59.* This is the logical order, because one goes to the street and then finds the number, but it gives to the American reader a curious sensation of mentally standing on one's head.

There is another set of abbreviations, known as the Dewey dates, as follows:

	Months			Days of Week		
Ja.	*Apr.*	*Ju.*	*O.*	*Su.*	*W.*	*S.*
F.	*My.*	*Ag.*	*N.*	*M.*	*Th.*	
Mr.	*Je.*	*S.*	*D.*	*Tu.*	*F.*	

These may be used in tables and in other places where very great condensation is necessary, but not elsewhere.

In general, much greater abbreviation is permissible in the tables, notes, and other condensed matter than in the body of the text.

III. TIME.

Statements of time should not be abbreviated in ordinary reading matter; *at half past two o'clock in the afternoon.* If the context makes it clear whether forenoon or afternoon is meant one may write:

at three, at seven o' clock.

This form is used statistically, in enumerations, in tables, and the like.

IV. OTHER ABBREVIATIONS INVOLVING THE USE OF NUMERALS.

The use of numerals and the spelling of numbers in full will be found treated at length in the Printer's Manual of Style (No. 42). As the use of the numeral is in a sense an abbreviation a few general rules may properly be given here.

1. Spell out ages;

eighty-two years and four months old.
in his eighty-third year.
children between the ages of six and fourteen.

2. Spell out references to decades;

in the early eighties.

The form *in the '80s,* is very objectionable.

3. Spell out numbers of centuries, of sessions of Congress, of military bodies, of political divisions, of Egyptian Dynasties, of streets, and the like unless lack of space renders the abbreviation absolutely necessary.

Twentieth century.
Forty-second Congress.
One hundred and first Pennsylvania Infantry.
Eighteenth Dynasty.
Ninth Ward.
Fifth Avenue.

In case numerals are used, Egyptian Dynasties are always designated by Roman numerals. Writers on Egypt usually use this form:

XVIII*th Dynasty.*

4. Spell out sums of money when occurring in ordinary reading matter in isolated cases:

That press cost five thousand dollars.

When several such numbers occur close together, and in all statistical matter, use figures.

Those three presses cost $2,500, $3,600, and $5,000.

5. Spell out round numbers, that is, approximate numbers in units of 100 in numbers of less than 1000 and in units of 1000 if the numbers are more.

An army corps numbers forty thousand men.
The Fifth Corps numbers 37,462.
There are about five hundred officers.

Write *fifteen hundred* and the like when the phrase is in common use, not *one thousand five hundred*.

6. Spell out all numbers, no matter how high, when they begin a sentence.

Four thousand nine hundred and sixty-four soldiers, 109 officers, and 10,000 civilians were surrendered with the fort.

7. Spell out in ordinary reading matter all numbers of less than three digits, unless they are of a statistical or technical character or occur in groups of six or more in close connection.

There are sixty cities in the United States with a population of 100,000 or over.
a ninety-ton engine.
five pounds of butter.
He lived only two years, one month, and twenty days.
He spent 137 days in prison.
A ratio of 16 to 1.
The death rate varies from 1 in 15 to 1 in 65.
Send home:
  2 pounds of butter
  1 pound of sugar
  ½ pound of coffee
  ¼ pound of tea
  2 pecks of potatoes
  1 pound of salt pork
  2 pounds of lard
  1 quart of milk

Treat all numbers in collected groups alike if possible, that is use either the long or the short form for all. If the largest contains three or more digits use figures for all.

They came in groups of 50, 80, 100, and even 200.

8. Express in figures as a rule decimals, degrees, dimensions, distances, enumerations, money, (but see 4 above), percentage, weights, and the like.

.542, 98°, 9 cubic yards, 37 miles, 24 pages, $1000,
6 per cent (or 6% but never six %), 175 pounds.

V. GEOGRAPHICAL ABBREVIATIONS.

Geographical names are ordinarily not abbreviated in text matter. The abbreviations in the subjoined lists are commonly recognized and may be used in lists, bibliographical matter, and elsewhere where condensation is desired.

UNITED STATES AND TERRITORIES

Ala.	Alabama	N. D.	North Dakota
Alaska	Alaska	Neb.	Nebraska
Ariz.	Arizona	Nev.	Nevada
Ark.	Arkansas	N. H.	New Hampshire
Cal.	California	N. J.	New Jersey
Colo.	Colorado	N. M.	New Mexico
Conn.	Connecticut	N. Y.	New York
D. C.	District of Columbia	Ohio	Ohio
Del.	Delaware	Okla.	Oklahoma
Fla.	Florida	Ore.	Oregon
Ga.	Georgia	Pa.	Pennsylvania
H. I.	Hawaiian Islands	P. I.	Philippine Islands
Idaho	Idaho	P. R.	Porto Rico
Ill.	Illinois	R. I.	Rhode Island
Ind.	Indiana	Samoa	Samoa

Ia.	Iowa	S. C.	South Carolina
Kan.	Kansas	S. D.	South Dakota
Ky.	Kentucky	Tenn.	Tennessee
La.	Louisiana	Tex.	Texas
Me.	Maine	T. H.	Territory of Hawaii
Mass.	Massachusetts	Utah	Utah
Md.	Maryland	Vt.	Vermont
Mich.	Michigan	Va.	Virginia
Minn.	Minnesota	Wash.	Washington
Mo.	Missouri	Wis.	Wisconsin
Mont.	Montana	W. Va.	West Virginia
N. C.	North Carolina	Wyo.	Wyoming

Foreign Countries

Aus.	Austria
Austral.	Australasia
B. A.	British America
Br. Col.	British Columbia
Can.	Canada
C. B.	Cape Breton
C. W.	Canada West (Ontario)
Den.	Denmark
E.	East (London Postal District)
East Isl.	Eastern Islands
E. C.	East Central (London Postal District)
E. I.	East Indies
Eng.	England, English
Fin.	Finland
G. B.	Great Britain
Glas.	Glasgow
Ire.	Ireland
It.	Italy
Jam.	Jamaica
Jap.	Japan

L. C.	Lower Canada
Man.	Manitoba
Mex.	Mexico
N.	North (London Postal District)
N. A.	North America
N. B.	New Brunswick, North Britain
N. E.	New England, Northeast (London Postal District)
Neth.	Netherlands
N. F.	Newfoundland
Norw.	Norway
N. S.	Nova Scotia
N. W.	Northwest (London Postal District)
N. Zeal.	New Zealand
Ont.	Ontario
Pal.	Palestine
P. D.	Postal District (London)
P. E. I.	Prince Edward Island
Per.	Persia
Port.	Portugal
Prus.	Prussia
Que.	Quebec
Russ.	Russia
S.	South (London Postal District)
S. A.	South America
Scot.	Scotland
Sc. Pen.	Scandinavian Peninsula
S. E.	Southeast (London Postal District)
Sic.	Sicily
S. Isl.	Sandwich Islands
Soc. Isl.	Society Islands
S. Lat.	South Latitude
Sp.	Spain
Sw.	Sweden
Switz.	Switzerland

Syr.	Syria
U. C.	Upper Canada (Ontario)
U. K.	United Kingdom
V.	Victoria
W.	Welsh, West. West (London Postal District)
W. C.	West Central (London Postal District)
W. I.	West Indies
W. lon.	West longitude

VI. NAMES.

1. Abbreviate *Saint* in names of persons, cities, streets, churches, etc.

St. John Chrysostom, St. Paul, St. Botolph Street,
The Church of SS (Saints) Peter and Paul.

The word *Saint* is now omitted in speaking of the evangelists, the apostles, or the church fathers.

The Gospel according to Luke.
Paul's doctrine of salvation.
Augustine's "City of God."

2. In technical matter (footnotes, references etc.) use *Co., Bros.*, and *ampersand (&)* in firm names and names of corporations.

The Rand-McNalley Co.
Macmillan & Co.
Harper Bros.
New York, New Haven, & Hartford Railroad.

In text matter not of a technical character it is better not to abbreviate.

Harper Brothers have published.
It was printed by the Rand-McNalley Company.
The romantic history of the East India Company.

Do not use *ampersand* except with names of persons.

John Brown & Co.
The Brown Printing and Publishing Co.

When railroad names or other long names are abbreviated, use no spaces between the letters.

N.Y.N.H. & H.R.R.
U.T. & F.C. of A.

3. Do not abbreviate *United States* except:

(*a*) in immediate connection with the name of an officer in the army or navy.

Capt. John Smith, U.S.A.
Lieut. William Brown, U.S.N.

(*b*) When it is part of the name of an organization.

First Regiment, U.S.V.

(*c*) When preceding the name of a ship.

U.S.S. Texas.

4. Christian names should be spelled in full in text matter, except in an original signature or when following copy in a quotation.

The following is a list of the accepted abbreviations of the more common Christian names.

Alex.	Alexander	Fred.	Frederick
And.	Andrew	Geo.	George
Anth.	Anthony	Herbt.	Herbert
Ap.	Appius	Hos.	Hosea
Arch.	Archibald	Jas.	James
Aug.	August, Augustus	Jona.	Jonathan
Benj.	Benjamin	Jos.	Joseph
C.	Cæsar	Josh.	Joshua

Cæs. Aug.	Cæsar Augustus	Matt.	Matthew
Cath.	Catherine	Nath.	Nathaniel
Chas.	Charles	Pet.	Peter
Dan.	Daniel	Phil.	Philip, Philander
Eben.	Ebenezer	Phile.	Philemon
Edm.	Edmund	Reg.	Reginald
Edw.	Edward	Richd.	Richard
Eliz.	Elizabeth	Robt.	Robert
Esd.	Esdras	Sam.	Samuel
Esth.	Esther	Theo.	Theodore
Ez.	Ezra	Thos.	Thomas
Ezek.	Ezekiel	Tim.	Timothy
Ferd.	Ferdinand	Wm.	William
Fran.	Francis		

Alex, Ben, Ed, Fred, Sam, and *Tom* are not always abbreviations and copy should be followed as regards the period. Any unusual abbreviations used by an individual should be followed in giving an original signature.

G°. Washington.

VII. TITLES.

1. As a rule titles prefixed to a name should not be abbreviated except *Mr., Messrs., Mrs.* (French *M., MM., Mme., Mlle.*), *Dr., Rev.,* and *Hon.*

Professor, Colonel, General and some others may be abbreviated when the initials of the name are used;

Professor Smith	*Prof. J. T. Smith*
General Grant	*Gen. U. S. Grant*

Hon. and *Rev.,* which are similarly used, need special attention as they are often used wrongly. The following is the correct use;

The Reverend John Smith (formal reference)
The Rev. John Smith (quotation or correspondence)

Rev. Mr. Smith
Rev. John Smith

Rev. Smith is wrong and should never be used except as any illiterate form may be used in a quotation. When the names of sovereigns are mentioned only occasionally such names may be given in full.

George the Fifth, William the Second.

When such names occur frequently, as in historical writing, they may be printed with Roman numerals without a period;

George V, William II

Other titles following a name are abbreviated in accordance with the following list.

A.B. or B.A.	(*Artium Baccalaureus*) Bachelor of Arts
Abp.	Archbishop
A.C.	Archchancellor
A.D.	Archduke
A.D.C.	Aide-de-camp
Adjt.	Adjutant
Adm.	Admiral
Admr.	Administrator
Admx., Admrx.	Administratrix
Adv.	Advocate
Agt.	Agent
Aldm.	Alderman
A.M. or M.A.	(*Artium Magister*) Master of Arts
Amb.	Ambassador
A.P.A.	American Protective Association
Asst.	Assistant
A.T.	Archtreasurer
Atty.	Attorney

B.A. or A.B.	Bachelor of Arts
Bart.	Baronet
B.C.L.	Bachelor of Civil Law
B.D.	(*Baccalaureus Divinitatis*) Bachelor of Divinity
B.LL.	(*Baccalaureus Legum*) Bachelor of Laws
B.M.	(*Baccalaureus Medicinæ*) Bachelor of Medicine
Bp.	Bishop
B.R.	(*Banco Regis* or *Reginæ*) The King's or Queen's Bench
Brig.-Gen.	Brigadier-General
Bro(s).	Brother(s)
B.S.	Bachelor of Science or Bachelor of Surgery
B.V.	(*Beata Virgo*) Blessed Virgin
Cantab.	(*Cantabrigia*) Cambridge
Capt.	Captain
Capt.-Gen.	Captain-General
Cash.	Cashier
C.B.	Companion of the Bath
C.C.P.	Court of Common Pleas
C.E.	Civil Engineer
C.J.	Chief Justice
C.M.G.	Companion of the Order of St. Michael and St. George
Col.	Colonel
Com.	Commander, Commodore
Corp.	Corporal
Cor. Sec.	Corresponding Secretary
C.S.	Court of Sessions
C.S.	(*Custos Sigilli*) Keeper of the Seal
D.C.L.	Doctor of Civil Law
D. D.	Doctor of Divinity
D.D.S.	Doctor of Dental Surgery
Dea.	Deacon
Dep.	Deputy
D. F.	Defender of the Faith
D.M.	Doctor of Music

Dr.	Doctor
D.Sc.	Doctor of Science
D.T.	(*Doctor Theologiæ*) Doctor of Divinity
D.V.M or M.D.V.	Doctor of Veterinary Medicine
E.	(*after titles*) Edinburgh
Esq.	Esquire
F.D.	(*Fidei Defensor*) Defender of the Faith
F.G.S.	Fellow of the Geological Society
Fr.	Father
F.R.G.S.	Fellow of the Royal Geographical Society
F.R.S.	Fellow of the Royal Society
F.R.S.A.	Fellow of the Royal Society of Arts
F.S.A.	Fellow of the Society of Arts
G.C.B.	Knight of the Grand Cross of the Bath
G.C.H.	Knight of the Grand Cross of Hanover
G.C.M.G.	Knight of the Grand Cross, Order of St. Michael and St. George
Gen.	General
Gov.	Governor
Govt.	Government
G.R.	(*Georgius Rex*) King George
H.B.M.	His or Her Britannic Majesty
H.M.	His or Her Majesty
H.M.S.	His or Her Majesty's Service
Hon.	Honorable
H.R.	House of Representatives
H.R.E.	Holy Roman Emperor
H.R.H.	His or Her Royal Highness
H.S.H.	His or Her Serene Highness
I.N.R.I	(*Jesus Nazarenus Rex Judæorum*) Jesus of Nazareth, King of the Jews
Insp.	Inspector
Insp. Gen.	Inspector General

I.O.O.F.	Independent Order of Odd Fellows
J.A.	Judge-Advocate
J.P.	Justice of the Peace
J. Prob.	Judge of the Probate
Jr. or Jun.	Junior
K.	King
K.A.	Knight of St. Andrew, in Russia
K.A.N.	Knight of Alexander Newski, in Russia
K.B.	King's Bench; Knight of the Bath
K.B.A.	Knight of St. Bento d'Avis, in Portugal
K.B.E.	Knight of the Black Eagle, in Prussia
K.C.	Knight of the Crescent, in Turkey; King's Council
K.C.B.	Knight Commander of the Bath
K.C.H.	Knight Commander of Hanover
K.C.M.G.	Knight Commander, Order of St. Michael and St. George
K.C.S.	Knight of Charles III, in Spain
K.E.	Knight of the Elephant, in Denmark
K.F.	Knight of Ferdinand of Spain
K.F.M.	Knight of Ferdinand and Merit, in Sicily
K.G.	Knight of the Garter
K.G.C.	Knight of the Grand Cross
K.G.C.B.	Knight of the Grand Cross of the Bath
K.G.F	Knight of the Golden Fleece
K.G.H.	Knight of the Guelph of Hanover
K.G.V.	Knight of Gustavus Vasa of Sweden
K.H.	Knight of Hanover
K.J.	Knight of St. Joachim
K.L.H.	Knight of the Legion of Honor
K.M.	Knight of Malta
K. Mess.	King's Messenger
K.M.H.	Knight of Merit, in Holstein
K.M.J.	Knight of Maximilian Joseph of Bavaria
K.M.T.	Knight of Maria Theresa of Austria

K.N.S.	Knight of the Royal North Star, in Sweden
K.P.	Knight of St. Patrick
K.R.E.	Knight of the Red Eagle, in Prussia
K.S.	Knight of the Sword, in Sweden
K.S.A.	Knight of St. Anne of Russia
K.S.E.	Knight of St. Esprit, in France
K.S.F.	Knight of St. Fernando of Spain
K.S.F.M.	Knight of St. Ferdinand and Merit, in Naples
K.S.G.	Knight of St. George of Russia
K.S.H.	Knight of St. Hubert of Bavaria
K.S.J.	Knight of St. Januarius of Naples
K.S.L.	Knight of the Sun and Lion, in Persia
K.S.M. & S.G.	Knight of St. Michael and St. George, in the Ionian Isles
K.S.P.	Knight of St. Stanislaus of Poland
K.S.S.	Knight of the Southern Star of the Brazils, Knight of the Sword, in Sweden
K.S.W.	Knight of St. Wladimir of Russia
Kt.	Knight
K.T.	Knight of the Thistle
K.T.S.	Knight of the Tower and Sword, in Portugal
K.W.	Knight of William of the Netherlands
K.W.E.	Knight of the White Eagle, in Poland
L.	(*after titles*) London
L.C.	Lord Chancellor
L.C.J.	Lord Chief Justice
Leg.	Legate
Legis.	Legislature
Lieut.	Lieutenant
Lieut.-Col.	Lieutenant-Colonel
Lieut.-Gen.	Lieutenant-General
Litt. D.	(*Litterarum Doctor*) Doctor of Literature
LL.B.	(*Legum Baccalaureus*) Bachelor of Laws
LL.D.	(*Legum Doctor*) Doctor of Laws

M.	Monsieur
M.A.	Master of Arts
Maj.	Major
Maj.-Gen.	Major-General
M.B.	(*Medicinæ Baccalaureus*) Bachelor of Medicine; (*Musicæ Baccalaureus*) Bachelor of Music
M. C.	Member of Congress
M. D.	(*Medicinæ Doctor*) Doctor of Medicine
Messrs.	Messieurs
Mgr.	Manager; Monsignor
Min. Plen.	Minister Plenipotentiary
Mlle.	Mademoiselle
Mme.	Madame
M.P.	Member of Parliament
M.R.	Master of the Rolls
Mr.	Mister or Master
Mrs.	Mistress
Mus. Doc.	Doctor of Music
Oxon.	(*Oxoniensis*) Oxford
P.C.	(*Patres Conscripti*, Conscript Fathers) Senators; Privy Counsellor
Ph. D.	Doctor of Philosophy
Ph. G.	Graduate in Pharmacy
P.M.	Postmaster
P.M.G.	Postmaster-General
P.R.A.	President of the Royal Academy
Pres.	President
Prov.	Provost
P.R.S.	President of the Royal Society
Q.	Queen
Q.M.	Quartermaster
R.A.	Royal Academician
R.E.	Royal Engineers
Reg. Prof.	Regius Professor

Rev.	Reverend
R.M.	Royal Marines
R.N.	Royal Navy
R.N.O.	(*Riddare of Nordstjerneorden*) Knight of the Order of Polar Star
R.S.S.	(*Regiæ Societatis Socius*) Fellow of the Royal Society
Rt. Hon.	Right Honorable
Rt. Rev.	Right Reverend
Rt. Wpful.	Right Worshipful
R.W.	Right Worthy
R.W.O.	(*Riddare of Wasa Order*) Knight of the Order of Wasa
Sec.	Secretary
Sec. Leg.	Secretary of Legation
Serg.	Sergeant
Serg.-Maj.	Sergeant-Major
S.J.	Society of Jesus
S.J.C.	Supreme Judicial Court
Sol.	Solicitor
Sol. Gen.	Solicitor-General
Sr., Sen.	Senior
S.R.S.	(*Societatis Regiæ Socius*) Fellow of the Royal Society
S.T.D.	(*Sacræ Theologiæ Doctor*) Doctor of Divinity
S.T.P.	(*Sacræ Theologiæ Professor*) Professor of Divinity
St.	Saint, Street
Supt.	Superintendent
Tr(s).	Trustee(s)
Treas.	Treasurer
U.J.C.	(*Utriusque Juris Doctor*) Doctor of both Laws
V.C.	Vice-Chancellor
V.D.M.	(*Verbi Dei Minister*) Preacher of the Word
Vice-Pres.	Vice-President
Visc.	Viscount
W.S.	Writer to the Signet

folio, quarto, octavo.

Beyond that they are usually abbreviated by using the Arabic numeral and *mo*, but without a period;

12 mo, 16 mo, etc.

IX. WEIGHTS AND MEASURES.

Abbreviate the common designations of weights and measures in the metric system, as well as other symbols of measurement in common use when following a numeral;

1 m., 5 dm., 4 cm., 2 mm., c.m. (*cubic meter*), *c.d., min.* (*minute*), *sec.* (*second*), *lb.* (*pound*), *oz.* (*ounce*), *yd., ft., in., A.* (*Anglestrom units*), *H.P.* (*Horse power*), *C.* (*Centigrade* [*Thermometer*]).

X. FOOTNOTES.

Authorities cited in footnotes should be specified in the following order:

1. The best known name of the author. Give initials only when necessary to distinguish between several authors of the same name. Set in roman lower-case unless otherwise ordered.

2. The name of the book in roman lower-case. If there is a Bibliography, or list of authorities attached to the book the names of all works referred to should there appear in full, but should be abbreviated in the notes. Otherwise, the name is sometimes written in full the first time it is referred to in a footnote and afterward abbreviated. If the book has but few references to authorities the names may be given in full in the footnotes especially when the reference is to the book as a whole and not to a particular paragraph. In such a case as this last the name is often printed in italics.

Always abbreviate uniformly in the same book.

3. The number of the volume in roman numerals of capital letters. No period.

4. The numbers of the pages in Arabic figures. If there are several editions varying in subject matter and paging the edition used should be specified. If the edition has been specified in the Bibliography this information should not be repeated in the footnotes. In books like the Bible, Shakespeare, Blackstone, or Milton, which have been printed in innumerable editions book, chapter and verse; act, scene and line; section and paragraph, or canto, stanza, and line must be specified.

Number of paragraph only	No. 68
Stanza only	st. 18
Page only	P. 213
Line only	l. 384
Paragraph only	¶ 34
Section only	§ 5
Chapter only / Canto only	xiv
Book only	iii
Book and chapter / Part and chapter / Book and line / Act and scene	iii 2
Act, scene, and line	iv. 3. 45
Chapter and verse / Number and page / Volume and page	II 34
Volume and chapter	IV. iv.
Part, book, and chapter / Part, canto, and stanza	II. iv. 12
Chapter, section, paragraph	vii. § 3, ¶ 4
Volume, part, section, paragraph / Book, chapter, section, paragraph	I. i. § 2, ¶ 6

In abbreviated references to the Bible or to the plays of Shakespeare use Arabic figures prefixed to the name to indicate part of succession of the book, play, or letter.

2 Kings II: 5
3 John 11
1 Henry VI, iii. 2. 14

The following excellently chosen illustrations of good methods in handling numerous footnotes in learned works are taken from De Vinne's "Correct Composition."

From English Past and Present, by R. C. Trench

[1] Guest, Hist. of English Rhythms, vol. I. p. 280.
[2] Hooker, Eccles. Pol. i. 3, 5.
[3] Craik, On the English of Shakespeare, 2nd edit. p. 97.
[4] Marsh, Manual of the English Language, Engl. edit. p. 278.

From Gibbon's Decline and Fall of the Roman Empire, Murray's edition of 1881 (8 vols. 8 vo)

[1] Orosius, I. ii. c. 19, p. 143.
[2] Heineccius, Antiquitat. Juris Roman, tom. i, p. 96.
[3] Jornandes, de Reb. Get. c. 30, p. 654 [p. 87, ed. Lugd. B. 1597].
[4] Ausonius (de Claris Urbibus. p. 257-262 [No. 14]).
[5] A. Thierry, Lettres sur l'Histoire de France, p. 90.
[6] Procopius, de Bell. Vanda., I. i. c. 7, p. 194 [tom. I. p. 341, ed. Bonn].

From Hume's History of England, Cadell's edition of 1841 (6 vols. 8 vo)

[1] Herbert, p. 431, 432.	[4] Burnet, p. 322.
[2] Collier, vol. ii. p. 176.	[5] 34 and 35 Hen. VIII. c. i.
[3] Stowe, p. 575.	[6] Mémoires du Bellay, lib. x.

The comma is often omitted after the period in footnotes. The abbreviation *ch, p,* and *pp,* may be made in notes, but not in text matter.

In lower-case text do not use *&c,* use *etc.*

By-laws are often printed with side-headings *Art. 1, Sec. 2, etc.* It is better to print the words, *article* and *section* in full in the paragraph where they first appear and to omit the word in subsequent paragraphs, using the proper figure only.

Figures used in illustrations to facilitate their understanding and explained in small text below the illustration or in the text matter itself do not have No. before them either in the illustration or in the explanation.

Figures and letters used as references to footnotes do not take a period.

Where two or more pages are specified in the text set them thus: *Pages 24, 25, 57* not *pp. 24-5, 57* nor *25-57.* When the reference is to several pages continually set *pages 24 to 32.*

When a period of time is expressed by the dates of two or more consecutive years, set thus: *1846-7, 1861-5,* when there is a lapse of a year or more, set thus: *1866-7-1869-70.* Do not abbreviate into *'66-'7-'69-'70.*

LISTS OF ABBREVIATIONS

The following lists of abbreviations will be found useful.

Scriptural Abbreviations

Old Testament (O.T.)

Gen.	Esth.	Joel
Exod.	Job	Amos
Lev.	Ps. (Pss.)	Obad.
Num.	Prov.	Jonah
Deut.	Eccles.	Mic.

Josh.	Song of Sol.	Nah.
Judg.	(or Cant.)	Hab.
Ruth	Isa.	Zeph.
I and II Sam.	Jer.	Hag.
I and II Kings	Lam.	Zech.
I and II Chron.	Ezek.	Mal.
Ezra	Dan.	
Neh.	Hos.	

New Testament (N.T.)

Matt.	Gal.	Philem.
Mark	Eph.	Heb.
Luke	Phil.	Jas.
John	Col.	I and II Pet.
Acts	I and II Thess.	I, II and III John
Rom.	I and II Tim.	Jude
I and II Cor.	Titus	Rev.

Apocrypha

I and II Esd.	Eccles.	Bel and Dragon
Tob.	Bar.	Pr. of Man
Jud.	Song of Three	I, II, III and IV
Rest of Esther	Children	Macc.
Wisd. of Sol.	Sus.	

COMMERCIAL ABBREVIATIONS

A1	Highest class or grade
Acct.	Account
Advt., Ad.	Advertisement
Agt.	Agent
Amt.	Amount
Anon.	Anonymous
Ans.	Answer
Art.	Article
Av., Ave.	Avenue
Bal.	Balance

Bd.	Bound
Bdl.	Bundle
Bds.	Boards
Bldg.	Building
B.O.	Buyer's Option
Bro(s).	Brother; Brothers
Chap.	Chapter
C.I.F.	Cost, insurance, freight
Co.	Company
C.O.D.	Cash on delivery
Cr.	Creditor
Dept.	Department
Do.	Ditto, the same
Dr.	Debtor
E.E.	Errors excepted
E.O.D.	Every other day
E. & O.E.	Errors and omissions excepted
Etc.	(*Et cætera*) and so forth
Ex., Exch.	Exchange
Exp.	Express
Fgt.	Freight
F.O.B.	Free on Board
H.	Hour
H.P.	Half pay, horse power
Incor.	Incorporated
Ins.	Insurance
K.D.	Knock down (*of furniture, etc.*)
L.P.	Large Paper
Memo.	Memorandum
Mfg.	Manufacturing
Mfr.	Manufacturer
Min.	Minute
No.	(*numero*) number
O.K.	All right

Payt.	Payment
Pd.	Paid
Per an.	(*Per annum*) by the year
Per cent	(*Per centum*) by the hundred
Pkg.	Package
Pl.	Plate, plates
Pref.	Preface
Rd.	Road
Rem.	Remarks
Rep.	Reports
R.R.	Railroad
Ry.	Railway
Ser.	Series
Sq.	Square
S.S.	Steamship, steamer
T.F.	Till forbidden

Miscellaneous Abbreviations

A.C.	(*Ante Christum*) before Christ
A.D.	(*Anno Domini*) in the year of our Lord
Ad lib.	(*Ad libitum*) at pleasure
Adj.	Adjective
Adv.	Adverb
Æt	(*Ætatis*) of age, aged
A.H.	(*Anno Hegiræ*) in the year of the Hegira
Alt.	Altitude
A.M.	(*Anno Mundi*) in the year of the world
An.	(*Anno*) in the year
An. A. C.	(*Anno ante Christum*) in the year before Christ
Anat.	Anatomy
Anc.	Ancient
Ang.-Sax.	Anglo-Saxon
Anom.	Anomalous

Anon.	Anonymous
Ap.	Apostle
Apo.	Apogee
Apoc.	Apocalypse, Apocrypha
A.R.	(*Anno regni*) in the year of the reign
Arch.	Architecture
A.R.R.	(*Anno regni regis*) in the year of the reign of the king
Arr.	Arrival
Art.	Article
Assoc., Assn.	Association
Astrol.	Astrology
Astron.	Astronomy
A.U.C.	(*Anno urbis Conditæ*) in the year of the building of the city of Rome
Auth. Ver. or A.V.	Authorized Version of the Bible
Av.	Average
Ave.	Avenue
B.	(*Basso*) Bass; bay; born
B.C.	Before Christ
Boul.	Boulevard
B.V.	(*Bene Vale*) Farewell
C.	Cape
Cæt. par.	(*Cæteris paribus*) other things being equal
Cap.	(*caput*) Chapter
C. or Cent.	Centigrade
Cf.	(*conferre*) compare
Ch.	Child or children
C.H.	Court House
Chap.	Chapter
Circ.	Circle(s)

Cit.	Citizen
Col.	Column
Coll.	College
Comp.	Companion, comparative
Cong.	Congress
C.Q.D.	Marconi Distress signal
D.B.	Domesday Book
D.C.	(*Da Capo*) From the beginning; again
Dec.	Declination
Deg.	Degree(s)
Del.	(*Delineavit*) he drew it
Dem.	Democrat
D.G.	(*Dei gratia*) by the grace of God; (*Deo gratias*) thanks to God
D.V.	(*Deo volente*) God willing
E.	East, Eagle(s)
Ea.	Each
E.B.	English Bible (common)
Ed.	Editor, Edition
E.E.	Errors excepted
E.G.	(*Exempli gratia*) by way of example
Elec.	Electricity
E.N.E.	East-northeast
Ent.	Entomology
E.S.E.	East-southeast
Etal.	(*Et alibi*) and elsewhere; (*et alii*) and others
Etc.	(*Et cætera*) and so forth
Et seq.	(*Et sequentia*) the following
Ex.	Example
Exc.	Exception
F., Fahr.	Fahrenheit (thermometer)
Fec.	(*Fecit*) he made it
Fem. or f.	Feminine
Fig(s).	Figure(s)
Finn.	Finnish

Fol. or f., ff.	Folio(s)
For.	Foreign
Ft.	Fort
Gent.	Gentleman
Ger.	German
Goth.	Gothic
Gr.	Greek
H.	Husband
Hdkf.	Handkerchief
H.e.	(*Hoc est*) that is, or, this is
Hist.	History, Historical
H.J.S.	(*Hic jacet sepultus*) here lies buried
H.M.P.	(*Hoc monumentum posuit*) erected this monument
H.R.I.P.	(*Hic requiescit in pace*) here lies in peace
H.S.	(*Hic situs*) here lies
Ibid. Ib.	(*Ibidem*) in the same place
Id.	(*Idem*) the same
I.e.	(*Id est*) that is
I.H.S.	First letters of ΙΗΣΟΥΣ, Greek for *Jesus*, or *Iesus hominum salvator*, Jesus the Savior of Mankind
Illus.	Illustrated
Imp.	Imperative (mood)
Incog.	(*Incognito*) Unknown
Indef.	Indefinite
Indic.	Indicative (mood)
Infin.	Infinitive (mood)
In lim.	(*In limine*) at the outset
In loc.	(*In loco*) in the place
Inst.	(*instante*) the current month
Int.	Interest
Interj.	Interjection
In trans.	(*In transit*) On the passage
Ion.	Ionic

Ir.	Irish
Irreg.	Irregular
Isl.	Island
Ital.	Italic
Itin.	Itinerary
J.H.S.	See I.H.S.
Jour.	Journal
Lat.	Latin, latitude
L.c.	(*Loco citato*) in the place cited
L.l.	(*Loco laudato*) in the place quoted
Long. or long.	Longitude
L.S.	(*Locus sigilli*) place of the seal
LXX	The Septuagint
M.	(*Meridies*) noon
M.	Married
Mem.	Memorandum, Memoranda
Mgr.	Manager
Misc.	Miscellaneous
Mo(s).	Month, months
M.S.	(*Memoriæ sacrum*) sacred to the memory
MS.	(*Manuscriptum*) manuscript
MSS.	Manuscripts
Mt.	Mount, Mont
Myth.	Mythology
N.	Noun, note(s)
Nat.	National
Naut.	Nautical
N.B.	(*Nota Bene*) note well
Nem. con or nem. diss.	(*Nemine contradicente* or *nemine dissentiente*) none opposing
N.L.	(*Non liquet*) It does not appear

N. lat.	North latitude
N.N.E.	North-northeast
N.N.W.	North-northwest
Nom.	Nominative
Nol. Pros.	(*Nol prosequi*) indicates in law that a complaint will not be prosecuted
N.S.	New Style (After 1752)
N.T.	New Testament
N.u.	Name(s) unknown
N.V.M.	Nativity of the Virgin Mary
N.W.	Northwest
Ob.	(*Obiit*) he or she died
Obj.	Objective (case)
Obs.	Obsolete
O.F.	Odd Fellow(s)
O.H.M.S.	On His Majesty's Service
Olym.	Olympiad
Op.	Opposite
O.S.	Old Style (before 1752)
O.T.	Old Testament
P. or pp.	Page or pages
Par.	Paragraph
Par. pas.	Parallel passage(s)
Parl.	Parliament
Part.	Participle
Partic.	Particle
Pass.	Passive (voice)
Pen.	Peninsula
Pent.	Pentecost
Perf.	Perfect (tense)
Pers.	Person
Pers. pron.	Personal pronoun
Persp.	Perspective

Phil.	Philosophy
Pinx.	(*Pinxit*) he painted it
Pl.	Plate(s)
Plff.	Plaintiff
Plup.	Pluperfect
Plur.	Plural
P.M.	(*Post Meridiem*) afternoon to midnight
P.O.	Post-office
Pop.	Population
Posit.	Positive
P.p.	Past participle
P.P.C.	(*Pour prendre congé*) to take leave
P. pr.	Participle present
P.R.	(*Populus Romanus*) the Roman people
Pref.	Preface
Pret.	Preterite tense
Pron.	Pronoun
Pro tem.	(*Pro tempore*) for the time being
Pr. p.	Present participle
P.S.	Privy Seal
P.T.O.	Please turn over
Pt.	Point
Pub.	Publisher
Pub. Doc.	Public Documents
Q.	Question
Q.B.	Queen's Bench
Q.C.	Queen's College, Queen's Council
Q.d.	(*Quasi dicat*) as if he should say; (*Quasi dictum*) as if said; (*Quasi dixisset*) as if he had said
Q.E.	(*Quod est*) which is
Q.E.D.	(*Quod erat demonstrandum*) which was to be proved
Q.E.F.	(*Quod erat faciendum*) which was to be done
Q.l.	(*Quantum libet*) as much as you please

Q. Mess.	Queen's Messenger
Qm.	(*Quomodo*) by what means, how
Q.p. or q. pl.	(*Quantum placet*) as much as you please
Qr.	Quarter
Q.S.	(*Quantum sufficit*) a sufficient quantity
Q.v.	(*Quantum vis*) as much as you will
Q.v.	(*Quod vide*) which see
Qy.	Query
R.,	Reaum. Reaumur (*thermometer*)
R.A.	Royal Academy; Royal Academician; Royal Artillery
R.E.	Royal Engineers
Recd.	Received
Rect.	Rector
Ref.	Reformation, reformed
Ref. Ch.	Reformed Church
Ref.	Reference
Regr.	Registrar
Regt.	Regiment
Rel. pron.	Relative pronoun
Rep.	Representative
Repub.	Republican
R.M.	Royal Marines
R.N.	Royal Navy
Ro.	(*Recto*) Right-hand page
Rom. Cath.	Roman Catholic
R.P.	(*Res Publica*) Republic
Ru.	Runic
S.	Solo (*In Italian Music*); South
S. SS.	Section(s), Saint(s)
S.a.	(*Secundum artem*) According to Art
Sax.	Saxon

S.C.	(*Senatus Consultum*) A decree of the Senate
S.C.	(*In Law*) same case
Sch.	Schooner(s)
Schol.	(*Scholium*) a note
Sci.	Science
Sculp.	(*Sculpsit*) he engraved
S.E.	Southeast
Sen.	Senate, Senator
Seq. or sq.	(*Sequente*) and in what follows
Seqq. or sqq.	(*Sequentibus*) and in the following (places)
Ser.	Series
Shak.	Shakespeare
Sing.	Singular (number)
S.J.C.	Supreme Judicial Court
S. lat.	South latitude
S.O.S.	Marconi Distress Signal
S.P.	(*Sine prole*) without issue
Sp. gr.	Specific gravity
S.P.Q.R.	(*Senatus Populusque Romanus*) the Senate and the Roman people
S.R.I.	(*Sacrum Romanum Imperium*) The Holy Roman Empire
S.R.S.	(*Societatis Regiæ Socius*) Fellow of the Royal Society
S.S.	Sunday School
S.S.E.	South-southeast
S.S.W.	South-southwest
St.	Saint, Street
Stat.	Statute(s)
Ster.	Sterling
Subj.	Subjunctive
Subst.	Substantive
Su.-Goth.	Suio-Gothic
Super.	Superfine
Superl.	Superlative

S.W.	Southwest
T.	Tenor (*in music*); (*Tutti*) the whole orchestra after a solo
Ter.	Territory
Term.	Termination
Theor.	Theorem
Tr.	Translator, transpose
Um.	Unmarried
Univ.	University
U.S.A.	United States Army
U.S.M.	United States Mail
U.S.N.	United States Navy
U.S.S.	United States Ship
U.s.	(*Ut supra*) as above
Vat.	Vatican
V.a.	Verb active
V. aux.	Verb auxiliary
V. def.	Verb defective
V. dep.	Verb deponent
Ven.	Venerable
V.g.	(*Verbi gratia*) for example
V. imp.	Verb impersonal
V. in.	Verb intransitive
V. irr.	Verb irregular
V.n.	Verb neuter
Vo.	(*verso*) left-hand page
Voc.	Vocative
Vol.	Volume
V.r.	Verb reflexive
V. tr.	Verb transitive
V.	Vulgate (Version)
W.	West, wife
W. lon.	West longitude
W.N.W.	West-northwest
W.S.W.	West-southwest

Xmas	Christmas
Zool.	Zoology

SIGNS

In addition to the abbreviations, strictly so called, there are many signs used in various kinds of composition. The most common are included in the following lists.

Monetary Signs

$	Dollar or dollars
cts.	Cents
Gn.	Guinea
£ (*English*)	Pound or pounds
/ or s	Shilling or shillings
d.	(*Denarius*) penny or pence
fr.	Franc or francs
c. (*French*)	Centime or centimes
m. (*German*)	Mark or marks
Pf. (*German*)	Pfennig or pfennigs
cr. (*Austrian*)	Crown or crowns
hr. (*Austrian*)	Heller or hellers
rub. (*Russian*)	Ruble or rubles
kop. (*Russian*)	Kopec or kopecs
kr. (*Danish*)	Crown or crowns
öro, öre	Oro or öre
£ (*Italian*)	Lira or lire
c. (*Italian*)	Centesimo or centesimi

Mathematical Signs

+	Plus
-	Minus

±	Plus or minus
∓	Minus or plus
×	Multiplied by
÷	Divided by
=	Equal to
≠	Not equal to
≡	Identical with
≃	Congruent to
>	Greater than
<	Less than
∼	The difference between
≎	Is equivalent to
: and ::	Proportion
∝	Varies as
≐	Approaches as a limit
∞	Infinity
∴	Therefore
∵	Because
...	Continuation
√	The radical sign
⊥	Perpendicular to
∥	Parallel
⌒	Arc of circle
°	Degree of circle
′	Minute of circle
″	Second of circle
∠	Angle
∟	Right angle
□	Square
▭	Rectangle
△	Triangle

Medical Signs

ãã	(*ava*) of each	ʒ	Drachm

℞	(*Recipe*) take	℈	Scruple
℥, ℥i	Ounce, one ounce	O	(*Octarius*) Pint
℥ss	Half an ounce	℥	Fluid ounce
℥iss	One ounce and a half	ʒ	Fluid Drachm
℥ij	Two ounces	m	Minim or drop

ASTRONOMICAL SIGNS

Planets

☉	Sun	⊕	Earth	♄	Saturn
☿	Mercury	♂	Mars	♅	Uranus
♀	Venus	♃	Jupiter	♆	Neptune

Phases

●	New moon	☽	first quarter	○	full moon
		☾	last quarter		

Zodiacal

♈	Aries, the ram	♎	Libra, the scales
♉	Taurus, the bull	♏	Scorpio, scorpion
♊	Gemini, the twins	♐	Sagittarius, archer
♋	Cancer, the crab	♑	Capricornus, goat
♌	Leo, the lion	♒	Aquarius, waterman
♍	Virgo, the virgin	♓	Pisces, the fishes

Aspects and Nodes

☌	Conjunction	☍	opposition
□	Quadrature	☾ or ☉	quintile
☊	Ascending node	✶	sextile
☋	Descending node	△	trine

ECCLESIASTICAL SIGNS

✠ The Maltese cross is used before their signatures by certain dignitaries of the Roman Catholic Church. It is also used in the service-books of that church to notify the reader when to make the sign of the cross. The ordinary reference mark [dagger] (the dagger) should not be used as a substitute.

℞ Response in service-books. The apothecaries' sign ℞ is not an entirely acceptable substitute.

℣ Versicle in service-books.

✶ indicates the words intoned by the celebrant.

Proofreader's Signs

No ¶	No new paragraph.
Run in	Let there be no break in the reading.
¶	Make a new paragraph.
✓ ✓ ✓	Correct uneven spacing of words.
℅	Strike out the marked type, word, or sentence.
↺	Reverse this type.
#	More space where caret is marked,
‿	Contract the spacing.
○	Take out all spacing.
[	Move this to the left.
]	Move this to the right.
⊓	Raise this line or letter.
⊔	Depress this line or letter.
‖	Make parallel at the side with other lines.
☐	Indent line an em.
⌣	Push down a space that blackens the proof.
x	Change this bruised type.
w.f.	Change this faulty type of wrong font.
tr.	Transpose words or letters underlined.
l.c.	Put in lower-case, or small letters.
s.c.	Put in small capitals.

caps.	Put in capitals.
⌄'	Insert apostrophe. Superior characters are put over an inverted caret, as, ⌄ᵃ ⌄° etc.; for inferior characters the caret is put in its usual position, as in ∧₁.
rom.	Change from italic to roman.
ital.	Change from roman to italic.
⊙	Insert period.
, /	Insert comma.
; /	Insert semicolon.
: /	Insert colon.
=/	Insert hyphen.
/—/	One-em dash.
/⁼/	Two-em dash.
ℨ	Take out cancelled character and close up.
Qu. or?	Is this right? See to it.
∧	Insert letter or word marked in margin.
‖‖	Hair-space letters as marked.
Stet	Restore crossed-out word or letter.
. . . .	Dots put below the crossed word mean: Cancel the correction first made, and let the types stand as they were.
⁀ae‿	Over two or three letters. Change for the diphthong or for a logotype, as *œ*, *ffi*.
≡	Straighten lines.
/////	Diagonal lines crossing the text indicate that the composition is out of square.
Out, see Copy	Here is an omission; see copy.

Corrections or textual improvements suggested to the author should be accompanied by the interrogation-point and be enclosed in parentheses or "ringed."

Corrections should always be made in the margin, and never in the text: faults in the types or text to be indicated only by light pen marks.

GENERAL OBSERVATIONS

There are many other signs and abbreviations used in works on the various sciences. Approved modern text-books are the only safe guides to the proper use of these.

In printing dialect, slang, and colloquialisms the only general rule is to follow copy.

Such abbreviations as *I've, you'll, 't'was, 't'is n't,* and the like are more clearly expressed when a thin space is put between the words.

Old Style contractions should follow the original even if special sorts have to be obtained for the purpose.

Abbreviations like *dept, dep't, gov't, sec, sec'y, sect'y, pres't,* and *treas.* are indefensible. Even in letter heads and the like it is better to spell out the words in two lines.

SUPPLEMENTARY READING

Correct Composition. By Theodore Low De Vinne. Oswald Publishing Co., New York.

The Writer's Desk Book. By William Dana Orcutt.

The list of abbreviations and signs in many of the principal dictionaries may be studied with profit.

Scientific text-books may be profitably used to study the abbreviations and signs used in mathematics and the sciences.

QUESTIONS

1. How and why were abbreviations used before typography?
2. How did the early printers use abbreviations?
3. What is the best usage with regard to abbreviations?
4. What is the general rule for the use of abbreviations?
5. What is the difference in usage between book work and some other kinds of printing?
6. What use of abbreviations do we find in certain special work and what may be done to make their use easier?
7. What are the rules for the use of abbreviations in dates?
8. What are the common abbreviations for the names of the months and the days of the week?
9. Give the Dewey dates.
10. What is the rule for ages?
11. How do we treat references to decades?
12. How do we treat numbers of centuries and the like?
13. What is the rule for sums of money?
14. What is the rule for round numbers?
15. How do we treat numbers when they begin a sentence?
16. What is the rule about numbers of less than three digits?
17. What classes of numbers are ordinarily expressed in figures?
18. What is the usage with regard to geographical names?
19. What are the rules for names?
20. What is the usage in printing titles?
21. How do we treat names of book sizes?
22. How do we treat weights and measures?
23. Give the order of specification in footnotes.
24. Where is &c not used?

25. How are by-laws treated?
26. How are figures used with illustrations?
27. What is said of the use of the period in footnotes?
28. How do we treat page references in the text?
29. How do we treat references to series of years?
30. How do we print dialect, slang, and the like?
31. How do we print such abbreviations as *I've, you've*, and the like?
32. What is said of certain improper abbreviations and how to avoid them?

The teacher should give frequent drills in the application of these rules. Sentences containing matter which involves the use of abbreviations and signs should be given out orally and the pupil required to write them out and set them up. The pupil should be required to explain by reference to the rules the use and the omission of abbreviations and the work should be criticised by the class or by the instructor with reference to the rules.

TYPOGRAPHIC TECHNICAL SERIES FOR APPRENTICES

The following list of publications, comprising the TYPOGRAPHIC TECHNICAL SERIES FOR APPRENTICES, has been prepared under the supervision of the Committee on Education of the United Typothetae of America for use in trade classes, in course of printing instruction, and by individuals.

Each publication has been compiled by a competent author or group of authors, and carefully edited, the purpose being to provide the printers of the United States—employers, journeymen, and apprentices—with a comprehensive series of handy and inexpensive compendiums of reliable, up-to-date information upon the various branches and specialties of the printing craft, all arranged in orderly fashion for progressive study.

The publications of the series are of uniform size, 5 × 8 inches. Their general make-up, in typography, illustrations, etc., has been, as far as practicable, kept in harmony throughout. A brief synopsis of the particular contents and other chief features of each volume will be found under each title in the following list.

Each topic is treated in a concise manner, the aim being to embody in each publication as completely as possible all the rudimentary information and essential facts necessary to an understanding of the subject. Care has been taken to make all statements accurate and clear, with the purpose of bringing essential information within the understanding of beginners in the different fields of study. Wherever practicable, simple and well-defined drawings and illustrations have been used to assist in giving additional clearness to the text.

In order that the pamphlets may be of the greatest possible help for use in trade-school classes and for self-instruction, each title is accompanied by a list of Review Questions covering essential items of the subject matter. A short Glossary of technical terms belonging to the subject or department treated is also added to many of the books.

These are the Official Text-books of the United Typothetae of America.

Address all orders and inquiries to COMMITTEE ON EDUCATION, UNITED TYPOTHETAE OF AMERICA, CHICAGO, ILLINOIS, U. S. A.

PART I—*Types, Tools, Machines, and Materials*

1. **Type: a Primer of Information** By A. A. Stewart

   Relating to the mechanical features of printing types; their sizes, font schemes, etc., with a brief description of their manufacture. 44 pp.; illustrated; 74 review questions; glossary.

2. **Compositors' Tools and Materials** By A. A. Stewart

   A primer of information about composing sticks, galleys, leads, brass rules, cutting and mitering machines, etc. 47 pp.; illustrated; 50 review questions; glossary.

3. **Type Cases, Composing Room Furniture** By A. A. Stewart

A primer of information about type cases, work stands, cabinets, case racks, galley racks, standing galleys, etc. 43 pp.; illustrated; 33 review questions; glossary.

4. **Imposing Tables and Lock-up Appliances** By A. A. Stewart

Describing the tools and materials used in locking up forms for the press, including some modern utilities for special purposes. 59 pp.; illustrated; 70 review questions; glossary.

5. **Proof Presses** By A. A. Stewart

A primer of information about the customary methods and machines for taking printers' proofs. 40 pp.; illustrated; 41 review questions; glossary.

6. **Platen Printing Presses** By Daniel Baker

A primer of information regarding the history and mechanical construction of platen printing presses, from the original hand press to the modern job press, to which is added a chapter on automatic presses of small size. 51 pp.; illustrated; 49 review questions; glossary.

7. **Cylinder Printing Presses** By Herbert L. Baker

Being a study of the mechanism and operation of the principal types of cylinder printing machines. 64 pp.; illustrated; 47 review questions; glossary.

8. **Mechanical Feeders and Folders** By William E. Spurrier

The history and operation of modern feeding and folding machines; with hints on their care and adjustments. Illustrated; review questions; glossary.

9. **Power for Machinery in Printing Houses** By Carl F. Scott

A treatise on the methods of applying power to printing presses and allied machinery with particular reference to electric drive. 53 pp.;

illustrated; 69 review questions; glossary.

10. **Paper Cutting Machines** By Niel Gray, Jr.

A primer of information about paper and card trimmers, hand-lever cutters, power cutters, and other automatic machines for cutting paper. 70 pp.; illustrated; 115 review questions; glossary.

11. **Printers' Rollers** By A. A. Stewart

A primer of information about the composition, manufacture, and care of inking rollers. 46 pp.; illustrated; 61 review questions; glossary.

12. **Printing Inks** By Philip Ruxton

Their composition, properties and manufacture (reprinted by permission from Circular No. 53, United States Bureau of Standards); together with some helpful suggestions about the everyday use of printing inks by Philip Ruxton. 80 pp.; 100 review questions; glossary.

13. **How Paper is Made** By William Bond Wheelwright

A primer of information about the materials and processes of manufacturing paper for printing and writing. 68 pp.; illustrated; 62 review questions; glossary.

14. **Relief Engravings** By Joseph P. Donovan

Brief history and non-technical description of modern methods of engraving; woodcut, zinc plate, halftone; kind of copy for reproduction; things to remember when ordering engravings. Illustrated; review questions; glossary.

15. **Electrotyping and Sterotyping** By Harris B. Hatch and A. A. Stewart

A primer of information about the processes of electrotyping and stereotyping. 94 pp.; illustrated; 129 review questions; glossaries.

PART II—*Hand and Machine Composition*

16. **Typesetting** By A. A. Stewart

A handbook for beginners, giving information about justifying, spacing, correcting, and other matters relating to typesetting. Illustrated; review questions; glossary.

17. **Printers' Proofs** By A. A. Stewart

The methods by which they are made, marked, and corrected, with observations on proofreading. Illustrated; review questions; glossary.

18. **First Steps in Job Composition** By Camille DeVéze

Suggestions for the apprentice compositor in setting his first jobs, especially about the important little things which go to make good display in typography. 63 pp.; examples; 55 review questions; glossary.

19. **General Job Composition**

How the job compositor handles business stationery, programs and miscellaneous work. Illustrated; review questions; glossary.

20. **Book Composition** By J. W. Bothwell

Chapters from DeVinne's "Modern Methods of Book Composition," revised and arranged for this series of text-books by J. W. Bothwell of The DeVinne Press, New York. Part I: Composition of pages. Part II: Imposition of pages. 229 pp.; illustrated; 525 review questions; glossary.

21. **Tabular Composition** By Robert Seaver

A study of the elementary forms of table composition, with examples of more difficult composition. 36 pp.; examples; 45 review questions.

22. **Applied Arithmetic** By E. E. Sheldon

Elementary arithmetic applied to problems of the printing trade, calculation of materials, paper weights and sizes, with standard tables and rules for computation, each subject amplified with examples and exercises. 159 pp.

23. **Typecasting and Composing Machines** A. W. Finlay, Editor

Section I—The Linotype By L. A. Hornstein
Section II—The Monotype By Joseph Hays
Section III—The Intertype By Henry W. Cozzens
Section IV—Other Typecasting and Typesetting By Frank H. Smith
          Machines

A brief history of typesetting machines, with descriptions of their mechanical principles and operations. Illustrated; review questions; glossary.

PART III—*Imposition and Stonework*

24. **Locking Forms for the Job Press** By Frank S. Henry

Things the apprentice should know about locking up small forms, and about general work on the stone. Illustrated; review questions; glossary.

25. **Preparing Forms for the Cylinder Press** By Frank S. Henry

Pamphlet and catalog imposition; margins; fold marks, etc. Methods of handling type forms and electrotype forms. Illustrated; review questions; glossary.

PART IV—*Presswork*

26. **Making Ready on Platen Presses** By T. G. McGrew

The essential parts of a press and their functions; distinctive features of commonly used machines. Preparing the tympan, regulating the impression, underlaying and overlaying, setting gauges, and other details explained. Illustrated; review questions; glossary.

27. **Cylinder Presswork** By T. G. McGrew

Preparing the press; adjustment of bed and cylinder, form rollers, ink fountain, grippers and delivery systems. Underlaying and overlaying; modern overlay methods. Illustrated; review questions; glossary.

28. **Pressroom Hints and Helps** By Charles L. Dunton

Describing some practical methods of pressroom work, with directions and useful information relating to a variety of printing-press problems. 87 pp.; 176 review questions.

29. **Reproductive Processes of the Graphic Arts** By A. W. Elson

A primer of information about the distinctive features of the relief, the intaglio, and the planographic processes of printing. 84 pp.; illustrated; 100 review questions; glossary.

PART V—*Pamphlet and Book Binding*

30. **Pamphlet Binding** By Bancroft L. Goodwin

A primer of information about the various operations employed in binding pamphlets and other work in the bindery. Illustrated; review questions; glossary.

31. **Book Binding** By John J. Pleger

Practical information about the usual operations in binding books; folding; gathering, collating, sewing, forwarding, finishing. Case making and cased-in books. Hand work and machine work. Job and blank-book binding. Illustrated; review questions; glossary.

PART VI—*Correct Literary Composition*

32. **Word Study and English Grammar** By F. W. Hamilton

A primer of information about words, their relations, and their uses. 68 pp.; 84 review questions; glossary.

33. **Punctuation** By F. W. Hamilton

A primer of information about the marks of punctuation and their use, both grammatically and typographically. 56 pp.; 59 review questions; glossary.

34. **Capitals** By F. W. Hamilton

A primer of information about capitalization, with some practical typographic hints as to the use of capitals. 48 pp.; 92 review questions; glossary.

35. **Division of Words** By F. W. Hamilton

Rules for the division of words at the ends of lines, with remarks on spelling, syllabication and pronunciation. 42 pp.; 70 review questions.

36. **Compound Words** By F. W. Hamilton

A study of the principles of compounding, the components of compounds, and the use of the hyphen. 34 pp.; 62 review questions.

37. **Abbreviations and Signs** By F. W. Hamilton

A primer of information about abbreviations and signs, with classified lists of those in most common use. 58 pp.; 32 review questions.

38. **The Uses of Italic** By F. W. Hamilton

A primer of information about the history and uses of italic letters. 31 pp.; 37 review questions.

39. **Proofreading** By Arnold Levitas

The technical phases of the proofreader's work; reading, marking, revising, etc.; methods of handling proofs and copy. Illustrated by examples. 59 pp.; 69 review questions; glossary.

40. **Preparation of Printers' Copy** By F. W. Hamilton

Suggestions for authors, editors, and all who are engaged in preparing copy for the composing room. 36 pp.; 67 review questions.

41. **Printers' Manual of Style**

A reference compilation of approved rules, usages, and suggestions relating to uniformity in punctuation, capitalization, abbreviations, numerals, and kindred features of composition.

42. **The Printer's Dictionary** By A. A. Stewart

A handbook of definitions and miscellaneous information about various processes of printing, alphabetically arranged. Technical terms explained. Illustrated.

PART VII—Design, Color, and Lettering

43. **Applied Design for Printers** By Harry L. Gage

A handbook of the principles of arrangement, with brief comment on the periods of design which have most influenced printing Treats of harmony, balance, proportion, and rhythm; motion; symmetry and variety; ornament, esthetic and symbolic. 37 illustrations; 46 review questions; glossary; bibliography.

44. **Elements of Typographic Design** By Harry L. Gage

Applications of the principles of decorative design. Building material of typography: paper, types, ink, decorations and illustrations. Handling of shapes. Design of complete book, treating each part. Design of commercial forms and single units. Illustrations; review questions, glossary; bibliography.

45. **Rudiments of Color in Printing** By Harry L. Gage

Use of color: for decoration of black and white, for broad poster effect, in combinations of two, three, or more printings with process engravings. Scientific nature of color, physical and chemical. Terms in which color may be discussed: hue, value, intensity. Diagrams in color, scales and combinations. Color theory of process engraving. Experiments with color. Illustrations in full color, and on various papers. Review questions; glossary; bibliography.

46. **Lettering in Typography** By Harry L. Gage

Printer's use of lettering: adaptability and decorative effect. Development of historic writing and lettering and its influence on type design. Classification of general forms in lettering. Application of design to lettering. Drawing for reproduction. Fully illustrated; review questions; glossary; bibliography.

47. **Typographic Design in Advertising** By Harry L. Gage

The printer's function in advertising. Precepts upon which advertising is based. Printer's analysis of his copy. Emphasis, legibility, attention, color. Method of studying advertising typography. Illustrations; review questions; glossary; bibliography.

48. **Making Dummies and Layouts** By Harry L. Gage

A layout: the architectural plan. A dummy: the imitation of a proposed final effect. Use of dummy in sales work. Use of layout. Function of layout man. Binding schemes for dummies. Dummy envelopes. Illustrations; review questions; glossary; bibliography.

PART VIII—*History of Printing*

49. **Books Before Typography** By F. W. Hamilton

A primer of information about the invention of the alphabet and the history of bookmaking up to the invention of movable types. 62 pp.; illustrated; 64 review questions.

50. **The Invention of Typography** By F. W. Hamilton

A brief sketch of the invention of printing and how it came about. 64 pp.; 62 review questions.

51. **History of Printing**—Part I By F. W. Hamilton

A primer of information about the beginnings of printing, the development of the book, the development of printers' materials, and the work of the great pioneers. 63 pp.; 55 review questions.

52. **History of Printing**—Part II By F. W. Hamilton

A brief sketch of the economic conditions of the printing industry from 1450 to 1789, including government regulations, censorship, internal conditions and industrial relations. 94 pp.; 128 review questions.

53. **Printing in England** By F. W. Hamilton

A short history of printing in England from Caxton to the present time. 89 pp.; 65 review questions.

54. **Printing in America** By F. W. Hamilton

A brief sketch of the development of the newspaper, and some notes on publishers who have especially contributed to printing. 98 pp.; 84 review questions.

55. **Type and Presses in America** By F. W. Hamilton

A brief historical sketch of the development of type casting and press building in the United States. 52 pp.; 61 review questions.

PART IX—*Cost Finding and Accounting*

56. **Elements of Cost in Printing** By Henry P. Porter

The Standard Cost-Finding Forms and their uses. What they should show. How to utilize the information they give. Review questions. Glossary.

57. **Use of a Cost System** By Henry P. Porter

The Standard Cost-Finding Forms and their uses. What they should show. How to utilize the information they give Review questions. Glossary.

58. **The Printer as a Merchant** By Henry P. Porter

The selection and purchase of materials and supplies for printing. The relation of the cost of raw material and the selling price of the finished product. Review questions. Glossary.

59. **Fundamental Principles of Estimating** By Henry P. Porter

The estimator and his work; forms to use; general rules for estimating. Review questions. Glossary.

60. **Estimating and Selling** By Henry P. Porter

An insight into the methods used in making estimates, and their relation to selling. Review questions. Glossary.

61. **Accounting for Printers** By Henry P. Porter

A brief outline of an accounting system for printers; necessary books and accessory records. Review questions. Glossary.

PART X—*Miscellaneous*

62. **Health, Sanitation, and Safety** By Henry P. Porter

Hygiene in the printing trade; a study of conditions old and new; practical suggestions for improvement; protective appliances and rules for safety.

63. **Topical Index** By F. W. Hamilton

A book of reference covering the topics treated in the Typographic Technical Series, alphabetically arranged.

64. **Courses of Study** By F. W. Hamilton

A guidebook for teachers, with outlines and suggestions for classroom and shop work.

ACKNOWLEDGMENT

This series of Typographic Text-books is the result of the splendid co-operation of a large number of firms and individuals engaged in the printing business and its allied industries in the United States of America.

The Committee on Education of the United Typothetae of America, under whose auspices the books have been prepared and published, acknowledges its indebtedness for the generous assistance rendered by the many authors, printers, and others identified with this work.

While due acknowledgment is made on the title and copyright pages of those contributing to each book, the Committee nevertheless felt that a group list of co-operating firms would be of interest.

The following list is not complete, as it includes only those who have co-operated in the production of a portion of the volumes, constituting the first printing. As soon as the entire list of books comprising the Typographic Technical Series has been completed (which the Committee hopes will be at an early date), the full list will be printed in each volume.

The Committee also desires to acknowledge its indebtedness to the many subscribers to this Series who have patiently awaited its publication.

COMMITTEE ON EDUCATION,
UNITED TYPOTHETAE OF AMERICA.

HENRY P. PORTER, *Chairman,*
E. LAWRENCE FELL,
A. M. GLOSSBRENNER,
J. CLYDE OSWALD,
TOBY RUBOVITS.

FREDERICK W. HAMILTON, *Education Director.*

CONTRIBUTORS

For Composition and Electrotypes

Isaac H. Blanchard Company, New York, N. Y.
S. H. Burbank & Co., Philadelphia, Pa.
J. S. Cushing & Co., Norwood, Mass.
The DeVinne Press, New York, N. Y.
R. R. Donnelley & Sons Co., Chicago, Ill.
Geo. H. Ellis Co., Boston, Mass.
Evans-Winter-Hebb, Detroit, Mich.
Franklin Printing Company, Philadelphia, Pa.
F. H. Gilson Company, Boston, Mass.
Stephen Greene & Co., Philadelphia, Pa.
W. F. Hall Printing Co., Chicago, Ill.
J. B. Lippincott Co., Philadelphia, Pa.
McCalla & Co. Inc., Philadelphia, Pa.
The Patteson Press, New York, New York
The Plimpton Press, Norwood, Mass.
Poole Bros., Chicago, Ill.
Edward Stern & Co., Philadelphia, Pa.
The Stone Printing & Mfg. Co., Roanoke, Va.
C. D. Traphagen, Lincoln, Neb.
The University Press, Cambridge, Mass.

For Composition

Boston Typothetae School of Printing, Boston, Mass.
William F. Fell Co., Philadelphia, Pa.
The Kalkhoff Company, New York, N. Y.
Oxford-Print, Boston, Mass.
Toby Rubovits, Chicago, Ill.

For Electrotypes

Blomgren Brothers Co., Chicago, Ill.
Flower Steel Electrotyping Co., New York, N. Y.
C. J. Peters & Son Co., Boston, Mass.
Royal Electrotype Co., Philadelphia, Pa.
H. C. Whitcomb & Co., Boston, Mass.

For Engravings

American Type Founders Co., Boston, Mass.
C. B. Cottrell & Sons Co., Westerly, R. I.
Golding Manufacturing Co., Franklin, Mass.
Harvard University, Cambridge, Mass.
Inland Printer Co., Chicago, Ill.
Lanston Monotype Machine Company, Philadelphia, Pa.
Mergenthaler Linotype Company, New York, N. Y.
Geo. H. Morrill Co., Norwood, Mass.
Oswald Publishing Co., New York, N. Y.
The Printing Art, Cambridge, Mass.
B. D. Rising Paper Company, Housatonic, Mass.
The Vandercook Press, Chicago, Ill.

For Book Paper

American Writing Paper Co., Holyoke, Mass.
West Virginia Pulp & Paper Co., Mechanicville, N. Y.

www.ingramcontent.com/pod-product-compliance
Lightning Source LLC
Chambersburg PA
CBHW081127080526
44587CB00021B/3780